The Eden Cage
~~ Dark meditations ~~

Saul Sangster

Four sequences of themed poems exploring darkness – especially the sorts of darkness that so often affect and afflict much of humanity.

True – there are many aspects of the human race that are wonderful, generous, creative and capable of love, but what of the other side?

What is darkness of the soul?
Where does it come from?
How does it reveal itself?

If you want poems of love and light, or even dark poems that have happy endings, you won't find them here. These are aspects of the darkness at the heart of mankind as seen through my eyes. (*And I'll brook no complaint about my use of 'man' . . . whoever heard of 'personkind?'*)

Indexes

BY SEQUENCE

DARKNESS DESCENDING	1
The beachcomber and ...	2
Behind the mask #1	3
Snake of souls (42/1)	4
The Hocus-Pocus	5
The Eden cage	6
Behind the mask #2	7
A touchstone for ...	8
Mason	9
On trend	10
Forbidden fruits	12
Darkness within, light ...	13
Nobody special	15
A day in your life	17
Snuffit	20
A working life (42/2)	21
Heads or	22
The edge	23
Russian roulette	25
Old soldiers	26
Detritus	27
Emergency admission	28
Pennies	29
Journey's end (42/3)	30
Ashes	31
Bonfire of possibilities	32

DARK GODS	33
Death of a hominid	34
Möbius morbidity	35
Salted hearts	36
god's pyramid	37

ALPHABETICAL

A day in your life	17
A solitary soul	84
A touchstone for ...	8
A working life (42/2)	21
All things	65
Altar stones	76
Amoeba	80
Ashes	31
Behind the mask #1	3
Behind the mask #2	7
Black	49
Bonfire of possibilities	32
Boxed in	104
Civilisation	54
Confession	102
DARK GODS	**33**
DARKNESS DESCENDING	**1**
Darkness within, light ...	13
Death of a hominid	34
Detritus	27
Do you want to know . . .	92
Door	91
Dust and love	98
Emergency admission	28
Forbidden fruits	12
Fragments and replicas	72
Fury and forgiveness	97
god's pyramid	37
Heads or	22
Hoo	74
In memoriam	105
Inheritance	66

BY SEQUENCE		ALPHABETICAL	
Inversion layer	40	*Journey's end (42/3)*	30
Service	42	*Life is precious*	85
Pigeonholes	44	*Life legend (Part 1)*	57
Prayer for the needy	45	*Life legend (Part 2)*	58
Man-maker	46	*Life legend (Part 3)*	59
Revisiting god's pyramid	47	**LINEAGE**	**51**
Looking ahead	48	*Looking ahead*	48
Black	49	*Man-maker*	46
---		*Mason*	9
LINEAGE	**51**	*Möbius morbidity*	35
The wound	52	*Nobody special*	15
Civilisation	54	*Old soldiers*	26
Song	55	*On trend*	10
Symbols	56	*Overdue*	95
Life legend (Part 1)	57	*Pennies*	29
Life legend (Part 2)	58	*Phobias*	61
Life legend (Part 3)	59	*Pigeonholes*	44
Phobias	61	*Prayer for the needy*	45
untitled #1 (emaciated ...)	63	*Realisation*	38
Sightseers at a disaster	64	*Revisiting god's pyramid*	47
All things	65	*Russian roulette*	25
Inheritance	66	*Salted hearts*	36
Statues	68	*Seed, flower and sexton*	100
The life, death & murder ...	69	*Service*	42
Stones	70	**SHEFFIELD JACK**	**83**
Fragments and replicas	72	*Sightseers at a disaster*	64
Hoo	74	*Snake of souls (42/1)*	4
Altar stones	76	*Snuffit*	20
untitled #2 (Belsenesque. ..)	78	*Song*	55
Amoeba	80	*Sorted*	93
---		*Statues*	68
SHEFFIELD JACK	**83**	*Stones*	70
A solitary soul	84	*Symbols*	56
Life is precious	85	*The beachcomber and ...*	2
The scholar	86	*The Eden cage*	6

BY SEQUENCE		ALPHABETICAL	
The fixer	89	*The fixer*	89
Door	91	*The Hocus-Pocus*	5
Do you want to know…	92	*The life, death & murder…*	69
Sorted	93	*The scholar*	86
Overdue	95	*The wound*	52
Fury and forgiveness	97	*Unbreakable*	87
Dust and love	98	*untitled #1 (emaciated…)*	63
Seed, flower and sexton	100	*untitled #2 (Belsenesque…)*	78
Confession	102		
Boxed in	104		
In memoriam	105		
Anniversary	106		

Paperback ISBN 978-1-7384576-4-9
Hardback ISBN 978-1-7384576-3-2
All poems © the author 2024

Darkness descending

The beachcomber and the fisherman

"There's nothing to find,"
said the beachcomber to the fisherman.

*"You can cast your net
as wide as you please.
The fish that you are seeking
have fled from the deep rolling seas."*

    The fisherman laughed
    and spat on the ocean.
    His spittle became surf on the shore.

    "They may have escaped me this time,"
    he said softly,
    "but I'll hunt them for ever more."

*"And what will you hunt
when you've caught them?"*
asked the beachcomber.
"What's left for you to do?"

    "Why," said the fisherman,
    as he sailed away laughing,

    "That's when I'll start hunting you."

Behind the mask #1
Knight's squire

Rumour came bareback
riding roughshod
over the occasional peasant;
generally moving at night
or in the early dawn
when light was insufficient
to give features to his face.

His shield,
protecting everything behind,
reflected nothing forwards.

He came on,
          invisible.

And was gone,
          laughing.

Squired by shadows.

---
*Partly inspired by René Magritte's paintings,
'Le faux miroir' and 'La Reproduction interdite'*

Snake of souls
42/1

He saw them approaching.
A snaking line of leaderless wanderers
heading his way.
The first in line said *"Follow,"*
but he stood aside as they passed,
watching them pretending not to see him
in ways that meant they saw him
only too clearly.

The last in line paused,
turned back,
and said, *"Join us and follow."*
But he stayed,
all alone,
watching them walk
toward prayed-for horizons:

an incomplete line;
a snake of souls;
an exclamation mark
without any stop.

He shrugged,
ignoring the way they had come,
and said *"Follow,"*
content in the certainty
that his shadow
would cling to every step.

The Hocus-Pocus

Ours is a world of filtered images;
of viewpoints thrown out of kilter.
A world in which perspectives are shifted
so as to confuse, mislead or bewilder.

A world in which what seems clear,
has been distorted by controlled illusion.
What we see, hear and choose to believe
is unreality that's the result of delusion.

Ours is a world in which the Hocus-Pocus
feeds falsehoods intravenously through needles,
implanting in our minds too easy an acceptance
that everything good, is free of all evils.

The Eden Cage

An allegory

What do you see when you look at the world?
Think of it as a drama you're being shown.
Shadows, shapes and flickering forms
including you in a group or alone:
seen on a screen as if in some film
whose narrative is not yet known,
even less, its eventual conclusion.
How can this life be your own?

Nothing pre-determined.
No audience to entertain.
You're in a company of random actors,
shackled to fortune in rattling chains.
Nothing rehearsed, scripted or set
No prompter to remind or explain.
The direction of every performance,
governed by capricious change.

The uncertainty of human life
means that dramas being staged,
are situations of consequence,
with you as player, masked and engaged,
improvising for no-one,
confined in your do-it-yourself cage,
an absurdly tragic comedy
of love, lust, hatred and rage.

----

*Yes – you're right. This is my version of the famous
'cave' allegory, re-imagined for the 21st century.*

Behind the mask #2
Faces

What mask are you wearing? -
The veil of belief?
An unveiled face without feature?
Or a collaged construction of symbols
to create the presence
of an unknown creature?

And when your mask is down,
what face is then on view?

Is it what you feared or hoped for?

Or might it even be you?

A touchstone for the pretending

Stricken by uncertainty
in a world of shadows
and shifting truths,
he stood fretfully in the wings,
watching and waiting
for the moment -

an intensity of contradictions
and dreamings
of something not so much
another self
as recognition of his true self.

A moment not of longed-for certainty
and sudden clarity,
but the dream
of both purpose and identity.

With a last dreadful breath,
he grasped the dagger
(*his touchstone for the pretending*)
and strode forth
towards Duncan's bedchamber.

Inspired by a quote from Willem Dafoe, when he was interviewed about his role in the film, 'The Reckoning' (which has nothing to do with Shakespeare). It was a phrase that instantly caught my attention and this poem popped out almost on the spot.

Mason

Grandfather made this mark.

Chisel in hand
he hewed the stone -
chasing a line
held by him alone.

An old man's fingers
and an old man's eye
worked together
to forever tie
stone to man
and him to me.
By neither time nor grime
can that bond broken be.

With my hand upon stone
I reach in and hold
onto warmth in the heart
of distant, ageless cold.

---

*Originally written to be read to a Year 5 class
in the grounds of St James' Church, Clapham,
during an educational visit to the area.*

On trend
A story for our times

So here it is -
the answer to your ills.
It's just like popping
a handful of pills,
or shooting it dissolved,
straight into your veins
as you immediately experience
the incredible gains
and fly ever higher,
as you forget every woe,
following the trend,
without feeling low.

It's wonderful.
It's Brill.
It's a smiley face.
You'll never regret it.
It's totally Ace.

Drop what you're doing
and take it from me:
it'll pass every test.
Just ignore the fee.

This is new.
It's the best.
It's on trend. Have a fix.
Overdose if you want to.
So why resist?

➤

You've got the habit,
You know you need it.
It makes you hungry,
so why not feed it?

The old ways are gone.
It'll alter your focus.
Open your eyes.
It's the Hocus-Pocus.

Each time you use it
your fears will grow less
as you lose sight of the truth
and the gathering mess
that will fester around you,
as you make matters worse,
until you find yourself
in an out-of-date hearse.

And then, at last,
you'll pay the fee.
Nothing in life
is ever free.
And your epitaph,
of course, will be
The Trend-follower's Curse:
your life described
in a single verse.

The fool in this grave
followed each fad and trend
and inevitably reached
this sorry end.

Forbidden fruits

The flowers of shadow wither in autumn,
shrivelling in expectation
of colder winds,
darkening nights,
and the juices
of soft fruit swelling
as their succulence
reach the point of bursting.

The fruits of shadow hang low on the branch,
within easy reach of little fingers
that know no better
than to reach up
to touch,
feel,
and taste
mysterious, forbidden temptation.

The fruits of shadow hang low and dark,
ripened not by sun,
but by an echo of footfall,
and faint, feather-light caresses,
shivering across delicate skin,
so easily broken.

The fruits of shadow fall to the ground,
wet and heavy,
ripe only when rotten,
ready to be trodden underfoot
and borne away as slurry,
their seeds stuck to the sole;
soon to root in fresh, fertile earth.

Darkness within, light without

Unfettered sunlight
shone down through each tree.
The forest floor was quiet,
like some becalmed, emerald sea.
A far-off rippling streamlet
tumbled unseen through ferns
while creeping ivy strangled
young saplings with vicious turns.

A pale blue periwinkle
bloomed softly amongst the trees,
its petals shivering gently
in every evening breeze.
A young child passed by, laughing,
her carefree day unplanned.
She plucked the periwinkle
and crushed it in her hand.

A man stood in the shadows,
the knife clutched in his fist.
He watched with burning hatred
as two lovers gently kissed.
He slithered through the darkness
and raised the bloodstained blade.
Fuelled by screams of terror,
he left them butchered and displayed.

The drunk lurched dull and senseless,
his thin coat ripped and torn.
His old shoes split and weakened.
His trousers bare and worn.
He came across the bodies.
Their blood flowed down the drain.
He picked their sodden pockets
and stumbled on again.

The accountant in his office
audited invoices yet to be paid.
Small suppliers could wait until last.
They couldn't sue or they'd lose his trade.
What did their suicides matter?
He could soon move on and replace.
His only concern, to maximise profits.
There were always others to fill their space.

The vicar in his pulpit.
The lecher in his lair.
Wherever people gather,
darkness is always there.
Its nature is often hidden:
no tail nor fiery breath ...
a natural part of being human
from birth, through life to death.

Need such things be inevitable?
Consider a child's sense of delight
in a rainbow, a butterfly, a song;
in life burning, blisteringly bright.
Do nature, nurture or luck
decide futures? That's unknown.
But the potential for darkness
lies in every soul,

                    every blood cell,

                        every bone.

Nobody special

Perkins the clerk
boarded the train,
his posture straight
and erect.
His razor-edged trousers
and bowler well-brushed,
showed Perkins
knew not self-neglect.

Perkins the clerk
ravished the girl
who sat
with thighs
open wide.
He did it again
through his Financial Times
and then,
once more
deep inside.

Perkins the clerk
spent his hours at work
filling in
nothing
but forms.
A meek little man
not given to plans
that would set him apart
from the norm.

➤

He made his way home
and raped as he went.
His saliva
slobbered for more.
He sat on the train
and did it again,
revelling
in fantasy gore.

Perkins the clerk
left the station
and walked
two blocks
to his single room home.
The gas burner
popped
as he lit it for tea.
Then he sighed once
and felt so
a l o n e   .

---

*Written in 1971 while observing passengers as
I commuted by train from Catford to Waterloo.*

A day in your life . . . ?
Stress

> *go on*
> *admit it*
> *you're totally knackered*
> *you feel as if your eyeballs*
> *have been imperfectly lacquered*
> *on the inside*

your head's fit to burst
and the veins in your brain
are flooding with acid
as a bloody great train
comes thundering from nowhere
and disappears unseen
into the hell of your gizzards
as deep as a ravine
where the waterfalls arc
and the white-water boils
hurling shattered detritus
along slippery coils

> *go on*
> *admit it*
> *you're totally buggered*
> *you feel as if your eyeballs*
> *have been coated and sugared*
> *like almonds*

you're being stretched on a rack
in full public view.
hung drawn and quartered
in a permanent stew
muscles and tendons
stretched tight as a bow
your ribcage a gibbet
killing you slow
your eyes disappearing
in the belly of a crow
while the jester still dances
and cackles below

> *go on*
> *admit it*
> *you're totally screwed*
> *you feel as if your eyeballs*
> *have been permanently glued*
> *wide open*

this way and that way
wherever you turn
there's only one lesson
that's left to be learned
the buggers'll get you
if they possibly can
so hurry back Baldrick
with a neat cunning plan
and bring if you wish
your old mate Black Adder
I'm sure he has a cure
for my slackening bladder

go on
admit it
you're totally canned
you feel as if your eyeballs
have been blasted by sand
for a year

And when you die,
guess who'll bear the cost?
Your own loving family
who will grieve for their loss
while paying the bill
for your burial or burning
(unless you've bought a plan,
knowing you're not returning.)
Your files can be tidy;
your plans a neat treat.
But when all's said and done,
you'll still be dead meat.

go on admit it
that some of the time
you've seen yourself
in the words of this rhyme

worrying
 isn't it

?

In time, references to 'Baldrick,' 'Black Adder' and 'a cunning plan' will become less familiar. Sorry, I can't help that. The TV series they come from are still regarded as classics in the 2020's and will (I hope) remain so for decades to come.

Snuffit

I'll not return. I'm not asleep,
so in a jar, my ashes don't keep.

When I'm dead, don't buy a coffin.
Take the advice of this gardening boffin.

Might I suggest a better thing;
a way my death could benefit bring:

Just put me on the compost heap
where potash and bonemeal I'll make quite cheap.

And though this thought might make you squirm,
just imagine the joy it will bring to each worm!

Then as fertiliser, my praises sing
when you lightly fork me over in spring.

You could, of course, build a funeral pyre
with me on top to fuel the fire.

My soul would rise in tendrils of smoke
to blot out stars and make neighbours choke.

But at least I'd go out in a blaze of glory
and the gardening mags would have a good story.

At least when I snuffit I'll be much less bother,
spread ten grams to the metre as potato patch fodder.

As your garden's best friend, I'll act as supporter:
eco-friendly as a nutrient transporter

Or as an alternative ecological lark -
use me as a mulch with composted bark.

Think of my ashes as feeding plants every spring
What better epitaph than helping bees on the wing?

A working Life
42/2

Live to work
or work to live?
Give and take
or simply give?

Get a life
or never get
any return
worth the debt?

Step in time
or step aside?
Say "*Enough's enough,
my brain is fried.*"

Look around.
What do you see?
Any possible way
in which you'll be free?

Live to work
or work to live?
When time runs out;
no more to give.

So give yourself
time for breath.
There's no time left
after death.

Heads or . . . . . ?

Turn the coin over
>	The tail and the head.
Turn the coin over
>	The living and dead.

Set the coin spinning.
>	Which side do you call?
Set the coin spinning.
>	Which way will it fall?

Let the coin wander
>	and stop where it will.
Let the coin wander
>	then wait 'til it's still.

Look between fingers.
>	Bets can be hedged.
What are the odds?
>	Is it a face or on edge?

Is it one chance in two
>	or one chance in three?
Or are you clutching at hopes
>	that just cannot be?

Which way has it fallen?
>	The tail or the head?
Which way has it fallen?
>	Are you living or dead?

Written in 1969   The radio DJ Alan 'Fluff' Freeman read it on his Saturday morning radio programme.

The edge

Rock-still and steady,
alone on the ledge,
standing silently,
looking straight down.
Surging seas and heaving surf
move shingle that chatters and drowns.
I lean against wind as it pushes me back,
until I find that perfect place
where, with arms outstretched,
I balance my life
on the edge
of infinite space.

Below me a seagull wheels and spins,
whiteness dissolved in the strand
where boundaries meet and worlds collide;
where waters reclaim the last land.
My gaze becomes focused on eddies and swirls,
on spirals that form and fail;
on foaming threads that ripple and burst,
leaving bubbles in a broken trail.

Closer and closer I stare at the signs:
the patterns whose thunderous beat
seems just within reach,
yet so far away;
the patterns that never repeat.
The wind is around me,
it's buffeting pressure
thrusts and urgently sings
as far below, emerging from surf,
a seagull twitches its wings.

The world is in turmoil.
The waves explode higher,
threatening to shatter the sky.
Wind becomes Storm,
pushing me back to a world
suddenly strangely awry.
As if in slow motion,
the waning moon dips,
disappearing forever from sight
as high above,
the stars go out,
obscured by a seagull in flight.

The core of this poem is based on a memory from my childhood when I went on holiday to the south coast of England and visited Beachy Head. It was a very stormy day with almost gale force winds blowing towards the shore. Foolishly ~ but memorably ~ I stood very close to the edge and leaned over to look straight down. Only the force of the wind kept me from falling.

Russian roulette

There is no point
in playing games,
when all is said and done,

Far better to try
a different sport
and put one bullet in the gun.

Understand,
there's just one way
to know if you have won.

Spin the wheel of fortune.
When it stops,
your time has run.

If you're alive
when the hammer falls
You can say, *"That was fun."*

Spin the wheel again.
When will the game be done?
Or is the game already won?

Old soldiers

Transient as morning mist,
wreathed by their own breath,
they returned.

Exhaling life with its memory
of comrades' lost
and lessons never learned.

Bent by age.
Baggy uniforms and medals.
worn with pride

Recalling friends
in mud-churned fields
who had bled, cried, choked and died.

Wandering half-remembered lanes,
bordering peaceful pastures,
vaguely familiar, yet unknown.

Knowing,
as they strolled amongst poppies,
that they were crushing old comrades' bones.

Detritus

in the doorway
clothed in shadow
she sits
not so much ignored as unseen

a lifetime's weight of lost innocence
and hardship
hangs like folds of skin
on thin skeletal bone

memories of abandoned dreams
windblown along the gutter

her litter of mangled mementos
separate and lift
before chasing each other down the street
like abandoned children

there's no legacy here
nothing for the future
worthy of a second look

nothing more
than food for the fly
and an easing of conscience
with a carelessly thrown coin

walk on by

Written after seeing a young, homeless woman sheltering in the doorway of an empty shop in Warrington city centre. She had obviously once been very pretty and was desperately trying to keep control of the few bags and items that were gathered around her.

Emergency admission

I never saw his face

I never knew him, nor his wife.
They meant nothing at all to me
until that day.

I watched them unload the ambulance
and wheel in the trolley.

> *(She followed so quietly,*
> *like a chalk shadow;*
> *not even pathetic -*
> *just Mrs. Nobody*
> *with a handbag.)*

None of this shocked or touched me,
not even the blood.

It was her cry -
cut short by a single sob.

Clinical.

Antiseptic in its purity.

Penetrating closed doors
at the end of the long white corridor.

Pennies

The ceiling, like a coffin lid,
hangs above the bed
as all the unsaid worlds of words
still clog the throat,
already dead.

Close each sightless eye with pennies,
the heavyweight coinage of fear,
and the unbearable burden of knowing
that confessions and regret
will both be buried here.

Nothing sanctified.
Nothing forgiven.
No redemption.
Nothing shriven.

Journey's End
42/3

Life, at the end, means nothing -
a flaring spark; a momentary thing.
The briefest of incomplete journeys
on fragile, damaged wings.

Some lives leave faint traces
in memories, ideas and names.
Others are dust in a moment,
even before the digging of graves.

And dust, as we know, will be winnowed,
as wind separates grain from grain,
until there's nothing left to be found.
Until nothing of you will remain.

As you have probably realised, the occasional subtitles of '42' allude to 'the meaning of life, death and everything' in Douglas Adams' "Hitch-Hiker's Guide to the Galaxy".

Ashes

A life lived.
A voice unheard.
Ashes in the wind.
A silent, unseen bird.

Bonfire of possibilities

From the flames
beneath darkening skies,
firefly sparks
swirl and rise
around an effigy
as numberless legions
pull torches from the fire,
held aloft as beacons.

Gathering together,
their light fighting the black,
they forge ahead regardless,
knowing there's no turning back.

As each torch is finally snuffed,
its bearer is left to dwell
on whether the last flaring spark
reveals nothingness,
heaven or hell.

Dark gods

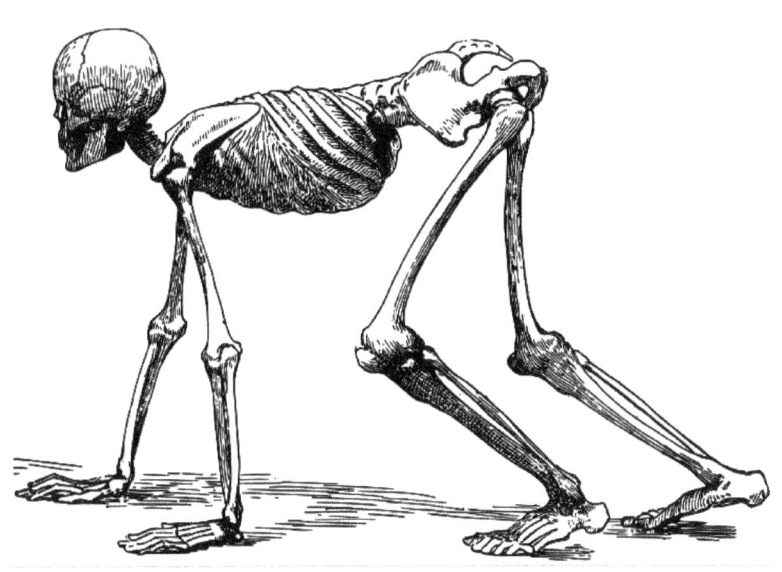

Death of a hominid

cold flecks floating in darkness
suddenly dimmed
as if obscured by a passing shadow
not of cloud
but of a desperately dreamed
Other

when the sky finally fell
there was nothing
beyond the perfect mercy
of Nothingness

Möbius morbidity
Infinite wisdom #1

Salted hearts

No true god
salts the hearts
of followers,
turning fertile and fallow
into barren dust-bowls
where seedlings shrivel
beneath the glare
of life's merciless sun,
or lets them reap death,
and destruction
with knife, bomb and gun.

god's pyramid

At the bottom -
the salt of the earth,
slaving away
for all they're worth.

Above them, layers
of managers trying
to make them do more.
Who cares if they're dying?

Above them, the bosses
piling on pressure.
Proving their value
is way beyond measure.

Above them, the bankers
wielding unheard-of power.
Hoarding billions like pennies
in each ivory tower.

Maybe above, maybe below
politicians gather
fuelling general disillusion
with self-serving ambition and blather.

Above them all, god,
watching the show -
wondering what the hell
is happening below.

And speaking of hell,
there's a basement level
where the homeless and lost
shake hands with the devil.

Realisation

Shock the monkey

They deprived him of everything
except food, water, warmth and a blanket:
      Touch.
      Comfort.
      Voices.
      Sympathy.
      Anger.
      And Love.

> *"He's only a monkey,"* they said,
> *"Just think about how much we can learn*
> *about ourselves.*
> *He isn't suffering.*
> *He doesn't know what that is.*
> *It's alright.*
> *He doesn't understand.*
> *He's only a monkey."*

So we watched him in his cage -
cowering in a corner,
curled and shivering,
as if his body was the battleground
for some loathsome, virulent fever.

> *"He doesn't understand,"* they said.
> *"It's alright.*
> *If he has concepts, they're different to ours."*

In self-induced ignorance,
and because I wanted to learn,
about what is in humans,
I believed them.

We watched the monkey -
curled and twitching in its corner,
clinging to blanket and frame,
as if now crushed
by some invisible weight;
as if terrified
of some incomprehensible horror
invisible to our eyes.

But I couldn't help but wonder
what it would be like
to be faced with an infinite immensity
of Nothingness,
without ever realising
that I had been denied the chance
to realise,
experience
or understand
the existence of
Mother
Family
Love
or Future.

Would I, perhaps,
in such hopeless moments of emptiness,
need to invent god?

Written 1975 when I first heard about Psychologist Harry Harlow's 1958 experiments with infant rhesus monkeys who were deprived of emotional support or their mothers. They were provided with a 'surrogate' in the form of a cloth or an inanimate wireframe model. Experiments suggested that the physical presence of a 'care-giver' did not need to be the one who actually provided food, emotional support and care. Later on some monkeys could not re-adjust. Many showed signs of autism, persistent rocking to-and-fro, or a refusal to eat. Several died soon after experiments ended.

Inversion layer

Infinite wisdom #2

god's eyes opened
to behold a whisper
of evaporating breath
swirling above valleys
littered with the bones
of faithful believers,
the jaw of each sightless skull
fallen open
as if death had arrived
without warning.

> *Had it been absolute loneliness*
> *or overwhelming enlightenment*
> *at the sight,*
> *at the end,*
> *the rapturous end,*
> *of each desperate illusion of heaven?*

god, with infinite wisdom,
knew he'd made a terrible mistake:
the infants had always been born malformed,
unmanageable,
unweanable.

But he'd left them to it
in the name of free will:

It was his unforgivable oversight.

Recompense was called for.

➤

The solution was obvious;
a final kindness
to those in such need:

Survivors' eyes were removed
before they were released
back into the wilderness.

When last seen
they wandered empty roads,
clutching empty begging bowls;
praising their father.

Service

The church door lay open;
a black archway
into a black womb
crotched by stone, snow and stars.

The people came;
heads on bodies,
shuffling forwards and into
the sterile candle-lit interior.

The door,
as at the other end of a long tunnel,
clamped shut behind them,
echoing in the cool stony silence.

Inside

they sank into stupor,
like droplets of darkness,
swimming together
into black unity.

All lay open before them:
their bodies and minds
spread-eagled on the cross;
labouring in darkness
to give birth
to that which drew them here.

➤

When it was over

the door opened
and, a little emptier than before;
a little more full;
a little nearer to death;
a little more determined to try again;
the congregation
was menstruated onto the snow.

Pigeonholes

Microbes.
Primordial origins.
Evolutionary paths.
We are what we are.
There's no escaping that.
We know where we came from.

But that isn't enough
until we have evidence
that underpinning everything
there lies something else
that isn't Happenstance
or mere Chaos.

We build multitudes of pigeonholes
and label each one, "Our maker."

Last time I checked,
they were all empty.

Prayer for the needy

The universe has Creation
without beginning or end.

Humanity fills nothingness
with a mythical friend.

Children have Santa
with reindeer and bell.

Then we give them god,
heaven and hell.

We teach them that prayer
can resolve most woes,

as if out there, somewhere,
there's a watcher who knows.

*"Our Father
who art ... ?"*

Man-maker

I don't know if it's true
or just a rumour,
that god has got
a weird sense of humour.

Who in their right mind
would make birds without wings,
or fish that can fly?

Who would make the dinosaurs,
only to let them die?

Who would make bats
who sleep upside down
or cats who chase tails
around and around?

Who would make a creature
who kills for power or pleasure,
who also creates music and art
of beauty without measure?

If there is a god,
my conclusion has to be
that the joker who made them
also made you and made me.

And if made in an image
that's the same as his,
then somewhere he's laughing
and taking the piss.

And if *that's* the case,
god's joke is the best,
because that would mean
he's as weird as the rest.

Revisiting god's pyramid

god, with head in hands,
is still watching the show.
Does he cry or laugh at us
in the garden, below?
Does he take a step back
to see the cosmos arrayed
in the hands of a child
playing with toys he made?

Does he see, in Creation,
a momentary lapse
when a mistake was made,
that causes its collapse?
Is that when god knows
he should have been more explicit
rather than staying invisible
as a nebulous spirit?

All of which proves
god's mistake is congenital.
The gift of self rule
is innately untenable.
Made in his image,
he can have no complaint
if Man worships himself.
It's an integral taint.

Rewind the clock.
Put Time in reverse.
Learn from the lesson.
Surely it can't get worse?

---
*My use of 'Man' is simply the traditional shorthand for hu**man**ity. It's not an anti-anything statement.*

Looking ahead

Life is terminal – but what about . . .?

When you are old, in your final days,
with weakened eyes and silver hair.
will memories blur and seem unreal?
Will you not remember who, what or where?

Will the young, as yet unborn,
understand fears you try to hide,
and will they need to turn away
to avoid embarrassment by tears you cried?

You know not yet of all these things.
You are young with life to live.
But fears will come when you realise
what it is that you'll have to give.

Will that be why you choose faith or belief
to understand life and death?
Will god be there to answer your prayers?
Or will black swallow your final breath?

The core of 'Looking ahead' was one of my earliest poems, written in early 1969

Black *(a meditation)*

For the sake of argument,
let's try to imagine black
as something real:
The darkness of sleep.
A space without echoes or light.
Something so hollow
and without dimension
that sound dies stillborn.
Strangled before birth.

A cell without windows
below the deepest dungeon
where the torturer is yourself,
and no matter how often you call out,
there isn't anything
that ever replies.
Not even echoes of your own screams.

But black isn't anything real,
unless we use the word to label colour
or emotion.

black is nothingness.
So absolute
that everything,
absolutely everything,
ceases to exist
except sound
taste
touch
smell
and fear. ➤

If black is anything, it's a metaphor
for the absence of everything.
black has no capital letter.
black isn't even an 'it'
black just isn't.
Total non-existence.

We live in the hinterland
between is and isn't.
Here today, gone tomorrow.

Is that why we need to say
        god is the light
        god is the sound
        god is everything
        god is all around
        god is all-knowing
        god is all-seeing
        god is infinite
our essence of Being?

That way, **G**od becomes an **It**
with a capital letter.
A candle in the black.
A pillar of strength.
A signpost to something beyond black.
An idea.
A symbol to reach for and hang onto
like grim death
in the face of ageless cold.

Lineage

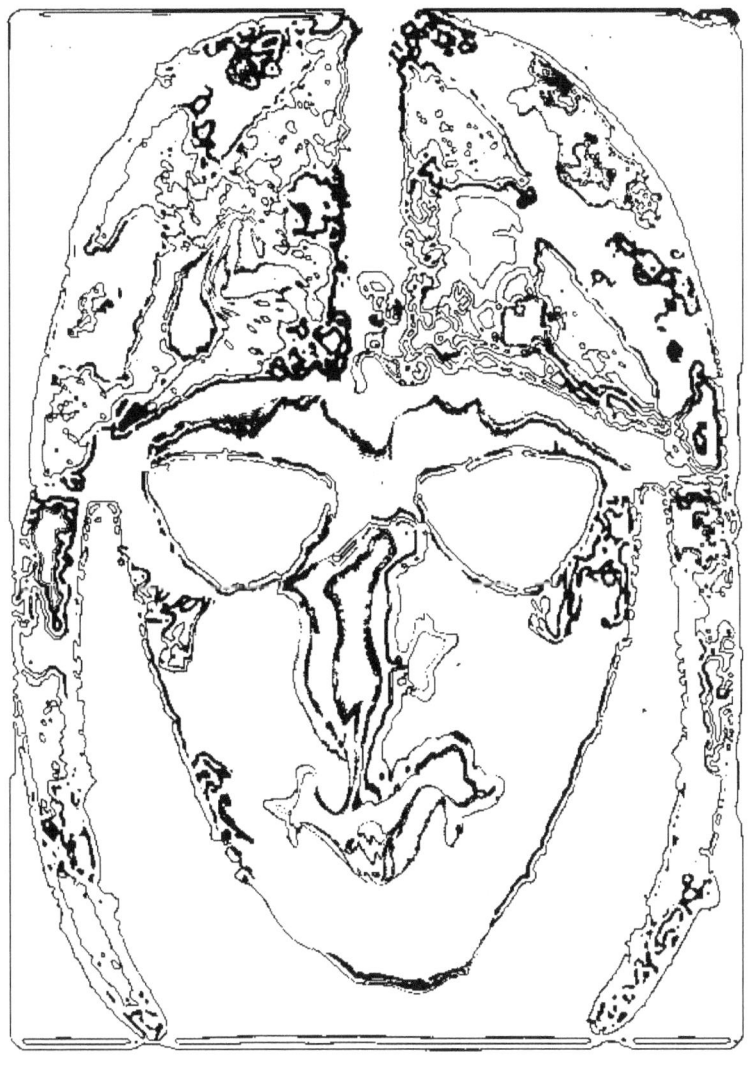

The wound

Once again,
the universe was torn asunder
by the act of creation.

Tissues exploded outwards.
Flesh and blood
erupted from the wound
as if in a bullet's path.

Ripped and flung aside
in slow motion.

Shivers of agony
juddered uncontrollably
along every nerve;
bringing fire
and the memory of birth
to a torn uterus.

In time
(*and of that there was near infinity*)
the wound scabbed
and seemed to heal,
but underneath the crust
raw flesh still ached
and bled.

                    Meanwhile ...

➤

Aware of a pain, but unaware why.
Aware of a need they couldn't ignore,
the outcasts of Eden played -
although, to be fair,
to them it wasn't play.
It was Life,
Fecundity,
and Death.

But still the wound bled,
forever thickening its scab,
slowing exsanguination.

Hopelessly,
helplessly,
they searched for ways
to live with the inevitable certainty
of death.

Eventually, of course,
the scab was torn apart.

The wound was revealed.

Unhealed.

There was only one remedy:
go back to the beginning
and try again.

Better luck next time.

Civilisation

        crouched like apes
        around a fire.

Fear

        hunkered down
        in tree-bound darkness
        all around.

Instinct

        flickered
        in stars and crimson ashes
        swirling upwards.

Ancestry

        howled and chattered
        at the moon
        behind its cage of boughs.

Future

        lurked behind eyes
        reflecting flames.

        Other smaller fires flared
        among branches, stems and roots
        still solidly locked
        to the jungle floor.

An ape

        put out its hand
        to the fire.

Song   *(Il requiem silenzioso)*

A first song.
A self-surprising duet
between the dissonant origins
of ensemble and language.

> *The song sung my Man is but a single song,*
> *sung by many singers,*
> *spread by wind and wave*
> *to distant lands.*
> *A single song of few notes*
> *trying vainly to catch the soul.*

A song of shock,
wonder,
and fear.

A brutal prelude to the incomprehensible
rattle of death.

Risen to crescendo, chorale and chant,
it fell back,
mortally wounded.
Fading back into silence.

> *The song sung my Man is but a single song,*
> *sung by many singers;*
> *a discordant improvisation:*
>
> *Heaven's despairing requiem.*

Symbols

Language, like superstition,
is tethered by the umbilicals
of lineage and tradition
to the womb, mystery
and time
of our spawning

and yet,
from the moment of that dawning,
successive ages have built the frame
and foundations
of knowledge, faith and myth
which, like it or not,
have become the core and spinal pith
of human tenacity,
doubt
and fear.

So we take as symbols,
ancient legends and beliefs;
weaving them as metaphors
to mask, explore, or
throw into relief,
the source of our uncertainties;

gaining, maybe, some new glimpse
or trace
or hope
of something to seek.

The symbol, however,
steadfastly rooted in ancient darkness,
simply grows another face
to be turned towards bleak horizons.

Life legend   *(Part 1)*
Written during a visit to the British Museum

The hunt

Two eyes met two.

Linked by the harpoon's short flight;
bound by the intent of one
to the frothing blood-choke of the other.
Blind to everything
beyond their individual universes.

Seeing
feeling
nothing
beyond the spear;
the bringer of harvest and final darkness.

No regret.
No recall.
Just a gentle fading;
a lowering of greyness;
falling towards the deep
and a last eternal closing of eyes
in a last eternal sleep.

All that had been experienced -
                                      gone.
All that had been instinct -
                               gone.
All that had been life -
                         gone.

Rotting to bones
and a momentary clouding of bloodied waters.

Life legend   *(Part 2)*
A new life

Gnarled hands carved me;
fashioned me by blade and eye
from tusks that once flashed
in icy waters.

The blade bit deep.
Shards of ivory
that had once ripped through flesh,
fell unnoticed, onto the floor.

Gnarled hands carved me;
the same gnarled hands
that had hurled the spear
and dragged my carcass from the sea.

In the flickering light
of my own burning oil,
those selfsame hands
now reveal who I am become,
then they abandoned me
to rot in awful darkness
beneath sand
on a desolate shore
because my shape
came not from the knife,
but from the release of legions
who have waited so patiently
in silences beyond life.

Life legend *(Part 3)*
The endless game

Bidden, we are moved;
not because we have the power to move you
by our strange shapes
or sensuous history,
but because we have become symbols
of your strategy.

You shut us out.
You have to
as you concentrate your will
when using us as players
on your battlefield of Mind.

You,
who cowered for centuries in caves,
or behind shields, stockades and walls,
peering into darkness
with candles screened from wind,
vainly seeking sight of your foe.

You,
the hunter,
whose instinct has lost its edge;
dulled by intellect,
and become blunt during unwinnable battles
for control of worlds beyond your reach.

We are merely your playthings;
your symbols of reason;
your pieces of a puzzle
whose pieces never quite fit.

Beneath your skin,
our fragmented shapes writhe to break free,
ready to bite through the umbilical
of your making.

Biding our time,
we move closer to the last few fires,
seeing ourselves reflected in your eyes.

Phobias

#1 She screamed.
Again and again
she screamed.

Her slender fingers dragging furrows of blood
across drained cheeks.
Her silent eyes
screamed
louder than any cries,
splintering air.

A spider, tense but still,
clung to her gaze.

A spider, older than memory,
weaved its silken web and waited
deep within the dark attics
of childhood.

#2 He stood, rooted.
Crushed by emptiness.

Then sank, whimpering,
curled like a foetus,
into prairie grass as it folded around him.

No trace left
as sirens of vacancy
sang him to sleep
as they sucked him dry,
leaving his husk to be winnowed
and whipped away by wind
across desolate landscapes.

#3   With throats suddenly dry,
     sweat oozed from every pore.

     They beat on door and floor,
     trapped in a darkness
     darker even than the inside of their skulls;
     gibbering to be released
     as deep within, at the heart of every cell,
     another greater darkness pulsed;
     rippling slowly outwards
     towards light
     and release.

#4   Older than dust,
     echoes swelled into chorus.

     Softer than mothers singing lullabies
     to their dead children.

     Howling like wolves beyond the skyline.
     Relentless as tap tap tapping
     on the other side of a locked door.

     A gelatinous eye at the keyhole.

     Blood upon the floor.

untitled #1

god
    emaciated
    roasted in the fires of Dachau
    marched with ice in his eyes
    out of Rome
    held with trembling fingers
    his own shattered arteries
    watching his blood
    drip
    drip
    dripping
    from bottles above beds
    ooze thickly
    and merge with mud
    knelt in line
    head bowed
    feeling his nape tingle
    awaiting the bullet's path
    opened his thighs for love
    and pushed inwards
    satiated his lust
    for life and death
    and wondered
    all the while
    when light
    would finally transplant the darkness
    of his own making

Sightseers at a disaster

Night lowered softly to the ground,
suffocating sight,
giving sound dimensions of vision.

They came through the dark -
soft of foot, fleet as cats,
padding,
softly padding
to eat and swallow
digestible night.

Then stopping.
Still as trees.
Tense in thickening pressure.
Distilling in this moment
the essence of vicarious pleasure.
Exhaling in their breath
living proof of every presence dissolving.

And now.
Here.
Now.
They press towards the light,
ravenously feeding
from the hollow bowl of night;
leaning forwards,
eyes agape,
feasting on and drinking in
the shape of young lives
mangled amongst the metal.

Needing, as do wolves beyond the flames,
to fill their bellies full of food;
to rip and tear and run
as if their very existence depended upon it.

All things

My year's memory,
brittle as bone
calcifies and turns to stone
beneath the dead weight
of fears and a gathering lake
of tears -
waiting to burst its banks,
filling every valley
with a lifetime's rain;
turning hilltops to islands
floating in a chain,
casting on each new shore
a crust of shattered jetsam,
leaving it there
to dry and crumble
and rejoin the waves
as dust.

        And dust to dust
        all things shall turn,
        as stone that once was bone
        shall turn.
        The dust of minute atoms
        swept but for a moment
        into a patterned pile of meaning.

        And bone that turns to stone
        shall crumble through the fingers,
        to be winnowed by wind
        and by the wind blown streaming
        and as dust
        return to the stars

Inheritance
Isn't this is what gods are for?

A funny thing, racial memory.
They say we all have it,
to varying degrees,
depending upon our lineage.

It goes a long way back, they say.
I suppose it must.
Back as far as the Eden Cage,
or beyond, even?

If we all share it,
then surely it must stem
from when we were all One
or, more logically, Two.
Does that sound rational?

So are we each the personal accretion of many?
How else could it have been passed on?
Left to linger in our minds?

That's if it's there, of course.

And if it is -
why should we have sole claim?
Why not the trees
and flowers;
wolves and cats,
lizards and worms,
bears, bacteria and amoebae,
molecules and atoms?

Who's to say we're the only ones,
living from moment to unconnected moment,
only to disappear into an eternity of forevers?

Perhaps all we ever learn or pass on
is eventually meaningless.

Perhaps our hopes are surrenderings
to seductive constructions of longed-for legacy,
offering the illusion of inheritance
and a belief that each life has purpose.

But isn't that what god's are for?
To promise us something for later on?
Even if it's only hell?

To make our lives subordinate
to limitations, laws
and reverence?

To make life and death seem
somehow reasonable?
Meaningful and bearable?
More than a mere coincidence
of self-sustaining processes
and accidental biological evolution?

To provide a pinpoint of light
to focus on in the black?

Statues

Michaelangelo believed
that in sculpting stone
he released only that
which was locked inside.

But when I look at statues,
pitted and eroded
by wind and time
and the effluent of man's progress,
I see figures melting back into stone.
Shapeless and formless in their own decay.

Parodies of man -
revealed like cancer
and the skeleton
beneath marble flesh;
truer in their decline
than ever they were
in days of their glory.

And finally,
when all evidence of the chisel is gone;
when all that remains
is the shapeless form
of raw rock -
only then shall we be shown
our true reflection.

Only then
will the artist have released
that which is locked inside.

The life, death and murder of Mr Eliot

Undimpled, the flesh is cleaved
by the surgeon's sterile blade.
Red welling blood is promptly swabbed
as the long incision is made.

The patient on the table
(etherised and unable)
screams awake through wounds new-raw
as his head, and that of the surgeon,
falls, surprised, upon the flaw.

Inspired by, and referencing,
'The lovesong of J. Alfred Prufrock' by T.S. Eliot

Stones

A ring of old grey men,
some standing
some leaning
some fallen -
all fixed silently
and forever
in the land's quilted landshapes
of shifting seasons,
all here for reasons
and forgotten meanings
from a time
when even the shape of time
meant less and far more
than for we who stand gaping,
framed in the lintelled door,
pausing on the threshold
stooped slightly
as if anticipating
the crush and fall
of stone hewed and shaped
by men who had time,
generations of time,
to erect on a moor
a ring of mute rock
which, now patiently leaning,
quietly waiting,
share only silence
with the wind's slow attrition;
accepting lightly
the change of seasons
and gathering grime,
forever adding
to the burden they bear.

They have witnessed the passing
of all that now lies sleeping,
generations notwithstanding,
untouched by the seasons
or the mind's shifting reason,
still gently breathing,
lying locked in our memories
and persistent superstitions;
skulking in shadows
behind thin bone walls;
restless and ageless,
still bearing scars
from when they were hewn
from the womb
and planted in strange earth.

Beneath their altar
they sleep on the floor,
huddled tightly together,
gently sweating and seething
like beasts in a cage
who wait and lie dreaming
behind a locked door.

Fragments and replicas
Written during a visit to the British Museum

Sooner or later everything is smashed,
dashed to pieces or shattered by blows;
buried by rubble or broken apart
to found a new order and give a fresh start
for anyone who will
  follow the guide
    and listen:
        a brief moment eclipses Assyrian might
        while the light of all Asia
        burns in one room,
        casting shadows of dragons
        upon Imperial Rome.

        Tombs of Egypt lie plundered
        as the eye of a Saxon bowl
        brims over with the soured wine
        of ancient ritual.

        Feast your eyes on leftovers.
        Pick over bones in a casket
        upon which hung the flesh of a saint.
        Lose your heart to a fragment
        that seems to speak straight from the past
        to the present,
        satiating your need
        to be a part
        of the body of Man.

Digest all you have seen
from times when mind, hand and eye
created, out of artistic need,
artefacts of indescribable beauty,
faith or brutality.

Each now displayed and devoid of its soul.
You can safely salivate and feast
until you are full.
Then stand back and label it

Art,
History,
Culture,
Ritual,
Belief.

Gratified by what you think you understand;
and to satisfy your need
for off-the-shelf evidence,
a souvenir from the shop completes your happy day.
Carried away like a disposable spare part.

Your very own fragment
of 'Objets d'art.'

There are 3 poems in this sequence that were written in situ at the British Museum during a visit organised by my English tutor, a wonderful man called Tony Aylwin. It's true to say that those poems, and Tony's enthusiasms, are a major part of how and why this sequence of poems ever came to be started. Far more than a teacher, Tony became a valued friend. He is much-missed.

Hoo
*Written during a visit
to the British Museum*

Eyeless,
awaiting no man.
Hanging in air.
Fearsome
only in the harsh vowels and cacophonies
of Bronze
and Iron.

A shape.
Nothing more.
An empty shell.
A chrysalis dried and hollow,
split by time
and the cleaving sword.
A moment's lending of fear
between the anvil
and grave.

Buried,
with honours,
and forgotten.

A moment's blending with darkness
whilst all else falls away
to dust
and shadows in soil.

Unearthed,
with honours.
A tarnished mask
from the age of bright shields
and dazzling cruelty.

A fragment of heritage.
Surviving,
because fire,
metal and stone
outlast the skin and bone
that used them
to fashion fear
into a likeness.

Altar stones

Blood-dark and silent
aslant in a stone cage
of ancient ribs,
the great heart lies drained and bare
as if abandoned by its body
or left until last
to rot and decay
to ashes and dust.

A heart in its skeleton
stained with life
and the fury of life -
bellowing in its day
for more offerings of prayer
to placate a hunger
fed by fear and need.

Silent now,
where all that is brought for slaughter
is the ravenous beast of superstition
straining against its coarse-woven leash.

Weakened by abandonment,
pacing side to side
with atrophied sight
in our bloodless hearts
and cages of crumbling bone.

Blundering to and fro,
stirring with its stride
the foul litter of its making.
Breathing as air
the stench of its own decay.
Feeding on the dark.

Searching for some sight,
some glimmer,
of returning light
and hope of release.

Escaping only when the ribs are bared
and the body,
bereft of spirit,
is gone.

Denied the let of revenge
or the cleansing of sores,
the blind forsaken beast
runs screaming to its lair
to sleep curled and shivering
like a kitten dreaming of claws.

untitled #2

The Belsenesque skeleton arches backwards,
jack-knifes forwards,
heads towards groin.

Loping stride becomes a jester's forward roll;
a snake's writhing
of side-pushed sand into ripples and coils.

Hands feather groin-wards,
fluttering like butterflies around a flame.

Eyes crush inwards beneath clamped lids.

The mouth opens,
splitting the face into a blood-red maw.

A snake of tongue rises upwards and out.

Screaming.

Silently,
as if the soul is being dissolved in acid.

As if its cry cannot escape the viscous fusion
of its being
and its dissolution.
Decomposing inwards.
A clouding, corrosive greyness.
Streamers of translucence.
Tapeworms
writhing,
curling,
and thickening.

Stillness.

Rigor.

The eyes twitch.

Muscles shudder.

Mouth shuts.

The quivering bone-bag stands,
sun-obscuring.

We see it glimmering through the skeleton;
a yellow diffusion in its cage of calcium
and parchment.
A halo of light around the beating heart.

Legs falter, then find their stride.
Hands swing in time.
The mouth smiles.

The eyes black.

Each a starless universe.

Life prevails.

Unquenchable.

Largely inspired by the horrific photograph of 9 year-old Phan Thi Kim Phúc taken by Nick Ut, as she ran, naked, screaming and burned, after a napalm attack by the USA in Vietnam (8/6/72)

Amoeba

A single cell -
no eye, no brain,
no belly, no bottom,
no nerves, no pain,
no fingers, no toes,
no knees, no joints.
Oh, poor amoeba,
what's the point?

No past, no future,
no good, no bad,
no dreams, no fears,
no mum, no dad,
no friends, no foes,
yet in your blob
there must somewhere be
the hand of god.

I think, therefore, I am.
I think.
Could it therefore be
you're the missing link
between that which was
and that which wasn't;
between that which exists
and that which doesn't ?

➤

Without a brain,
you can't ask why.
Do you even know
that you live and die?
All you do
is slither and slide
until it's time
to subdivide.

Or am I wrong?
Should I look anew?
Do amoebae have
a different view?
Are you each a part
of some unimaginable whole?
A single cell.
A simple soul?

Sheffield Jack

A separate, but not altogether unrelated, sequence of poems

A solitary soul

August the Eighth.
Born without love.
Died in hate.
Lived his life as if he couldn't wait.

First light of day, kicking and screaming.
Fought his way from nightmare to breathing.
Fell on the floor, gasping for air.
Not knowing nor needing anyone there.

A solitary soul, defenceless and dying.
Each breath a rasp.
One heave away from the final gasp.
Saved by the cut of some unknown hand.
A moment's kindness
in a cruel new land.

If only he'd known, he could have locked it away.
A spark of light to keep beasts at bay.

But too soon, too late.
The knife and the knot had sealed his fate;
bound him as tight
as any born hunter
is bound to their prey,
as lightning is bound
to endless thunder.

Life is precious

'Mother unknown.'
'Father unknown.'
    A baby boy. Four pounds four.
    The certificate was simple.
    It could say no more.

'No known address.'
    The tenth that month.
    Abandoned and bagged.
    Tenth letter 'J'.
    'Jack' scribbled and tagged.

'Sheffield born'
    Given that name as his own.
    Poor little bleeder.
    The nurse was busy.
    He didn't need her.
    A natural survivor.
    An instinctive feeder.

"Nothing comes of nothing",
    that's what they said.

"Leave him to die. He's better off dead."
    It wasn't so much that they didn't care.
    He was just one too many.
    Life's not always fair.

The scholar

Want to know what school's for?

It's for rehearsing,
for practising,
for learning what's useful.

It's not for passing exams.
It's for taking time out,
for spotting rules to bend.

Rules aren't for obeying.
They're prison bars.
They're lock-ups for losers.

Keys aren't important.
Locks are there for breaking,
for getting past defences.

School's a charity shop
of donated hand-me-downs
that rarely fit.

Only two things you can do:
grow into them,
or rip them to shreds.

School is a hiding place.
It gives you time to look round.
Time to get ready.

It's camouflage for the chrysalis.

Unbreakable

Jack Boy's got a temper.
Fists as hard as brick.
If he doesn't get his way,
he'll sulk and frown and kick.
He glowers at the floor
and screws his face up tight,
and you know that come 3 o'clock,
he'll be looking for a fight.

Jack Boy's got a temper.
and moods he can't control.
If he doesn't get his way,
he'll crawl into a hole
or he'll spit like a venomous snake
as he sweeps schoolbooks off the shelf
If anyone tries to talk him down,
he'll scream, *"Go fuck yourself"*.

His battleground is the playground.
He's the king of kicks and gobbing.
When dragged away by teachers,
he says he's sorry and practices sobbing.
When he gets himself in trouble,
there's only one thing to do,
so he bangs his head against the wall
until his forehead's black and blue.

➤

Jack Boy's got a temper.
It makes him cry at night.
If he thinks you even care,
he goes to bed for spite.
He screams into his pillow,
but there's no-one there to hear.
There's no voice, no hand, no kiss
to take away the fear.

Ghosts of raging fury
haunt him when he sleeps.
Curled like a foetus,
he moans as nightmares creep
and snuffle through the litter
of a day that's done and died.
Black shadows of his terror
leave nowhere left to hide.

In every dreaded nightmare,
his fists are hard as brick.
Every challenge is answered
with hit and bite and kick.
Survival means just one thing –
to soak up every hurt,
worn with pride like a tattoo
or bloodstains left in dirt.

Who cares what others think?
Who care what others see?
Jack Boy's got a temper.
That's his guarantee.
None will ever get close.
None will penetrate his guard.
Like the finest Sheffield steel,
unbreakable and hard.

The fixer

Not for him, the life of a dreamer.
He's a hard-faced,
mean-eyed,
devious schemer.

He'll swear through his teeth,
cross his heart and die.
It wasn't him.
He wouldn't lie.

He's always in trouble.
Always getting the blame.
It doesn't take long
until he masters the game.

A tale told here.
A tale told there.
No-one dares snitch.
They wouldn't dare.

A whispered lie
to teachers who struggle.
It's easier to believe him
and save all the trouble.

> *"Can't you see, Sir,*
> *a much better way*
> *whenever there's trouble*
> *is to stop me and say,*
> *'Find out who did it,*
> *and tip me the wink.'*
> *It's our little secret.*
> *Well, what do you think?"*

➤

Best turn a blind eye
to the need for proof.
Just go to him.
He'll get you the truth.

You'll have no more problems.
That's guaranteed.

> *"We'll work well together.*
> *I'm glad that's agreed.*
> *I'll help you, Sir,*
> *catch the ones who did it.*
> *I'll fix it myself.*
> *It'll just take a minute.*
> *A whispered threat*
> *in the bogs or sheds.*
> *A quick confession.*
> *There, just like I said."*

The word goes round.
Jack's not to be trusted.
Better not tell the truth
or your nose gets busted.

Lessons are learned.
That's what school is for.
He passes with honours.
Sheffield Jack's law.

Door

Everyone, sometime,
has a moment in which
a single decision acts
like a single switch
and from that moment on,
life's succession of scenes
are beyond control,
despite any dreams.

 "He's on his own.
There's no more room".
His life defined.
Even in the womb.

From that moment on,
Sheffield Jack
gave never a thought to turning back.

A baby.
A boy.
A life-hardened man.
He needed no-one.
He needed no plan.

The world was his.
There for the taking
The world was his.
There for the making.

His life was his.
There was nothing more.
There was no reason to care.
He kicked open the door.

Do you want to know
what love is?

Keep away from Jack Boy.
      Get to know his name.
A thug and villain.
      Never gets the blame.
Can't speak without lying.
      He's always exactly the same:
like something wild
      that won't or can't be tamed.

It's as if he needs
      to enjoy another's pains.
I've no idea what he feels,
      nor what he ever gains
by flushing her smiles
      down his filthy drain.
His mark is her blood,
      a permanent loving stain.

Hers is an innocent soul
      silently struggling in vain.
Jack leaves her alone to endure
      being unwanted, scarred and maimed.
For Jack it's very simple,
      no question or doubts remain.
He knows she'll always be willing
      every time he calls her name.

Love is not for Loving's sake.
Love is something to hold and break.

Sorted

Hard as steel,
he forged his name.
Everyone knew Sheffield Jack.
Everyone knew his game.

He ground lives down
on the wheel of his hate.
Honed, tempered and sharpened it
in a battleground estate.

A broken bottle or a broken bone?
Everything's easily sorted.
Whatever's to hand.
Mercy is easily aborted.

A show of emotion?
You must be joking.
Laughter's the sound
they make when they're choking.

Blood on the sheets
is his tattoo of love.
But for the touch of tenderness
Jack wears a glove.

Never mind the bruises,
they'll disappear.
Just keep your distance
and soak up the fear.

Life's sorted --
iron bars and steel.
Anything else
is for others to feel.

Life's not a gift,
it's a curse in the making.
An unwanted possession
for taking and breaking.

Hard as the steel
from furnaces long cold,
Jack clawed clear of the rut;
crawled clear of the hole.

Life only really begins
when you get your cut.

Overdue

He remembered the torment.
Those nightmares were never his!
Childhood memories of waiting in darkness
for whispers and that first cold kiss.
A white-knuckle ride of subjection
with love at the end of a fist.
Those fears gestating until waters
broke as he learned to resist.

If nothing else, a lesson had been learned:
the best form of defence is attack.
Don't ever allow dreams to be born,
and never ever think of turning back
to friends half won and irretrievably lost
in the shadowlands of play;
nor of urgency in the darkness,
or being lonely throughout the day.

Sheffield Jack had a special cancer:
a pregnant tumour in his soul.
It kicked and writhed in moments of peace.
A formless pain becoming whole.
And like all good mammals in this condition,
he did what he had to do,
offering nightmares and terror as nourishment.
He had to eat enough for two.

➤

Warmth
and Love
and Family
were Otherworlds, vile and obscene.
Words in a foreign language,
from hated countries he had never seen.
Long-since forgotten, one moment of care,
a crippled foetus, deformed by life,
its love-giving umbilical severed
by gloved hands and a nurse's knife.

Fury and forgiveness

Again and again
he shook with a near-epileptic seizure.
> *Don't hold back.*
> *Go on.*
> *Hit out.*
> *Hurt.*
> *Attack.*

Something inside
wanted the world damaged.
Bleeding.
Dead.
Never giving him a voice or choice of his own.

A fury of fire that wouldn't be calmed
until someone
or something
had been fatally harmed.
Even if it was him.

That's what life was all about.

That had been his only absolution
until now:
> a need never known before
> as if something, left so long to starve,
> was whimpering in the darkness;
> scratching at the door
> afraid of the light,
> afraid of something beyond the pain,
> afraid of something unknown and more.
> Afraid of being afraid.

Dust and love

"I love you," Jack had tried to say,
as rains ran down the glass.
Cataracts of loneliness
obscuring rage behind the mask.

The fornication that followed
came as pain and lust coalesced.
Love bled from each new rupture
in pale, once-innocent flesh.

Impotent fury soaked into walls
adding to histories of gaping wounds
reflected in fragments of mirrors;
rainbows edged with delicate perfumes.

The cloying reek of the beast's true lair
and the coppery scent of satisfied lust
quickly became an amalgamation
of scribblings in gatherings of dust.

"I love you," Jack had tried to say,
as if it was something meant to be said;
a game to be played to make it more real
when flesh surrendered to flesh long dead.

"I love you," Jack had managed to say,
still not sure of what those words meant
when, instead of bruises and submission,
there was just warmth and a flowery scent.

He lay on the bed, gasping for air,
unprepared for the touch of a hand
that didn't reach out to scratch or defend;
which didn't label him one of the damned.

Barely acknowledging the touch of soft skin
or the lips cleansing blood with each kiss.
He cursed himself whilst hating the pain
of punching walls with balled-up fists.

"I love you'" Jack had tried to say.
Words with no meaning when said.
"*I love you, Jack,*" were the words he heard,
unable to gloat at the tears she shed.

Seed, flower and sexton

A seed,
hard and opaque,
black as fossilised coal
fuelling furnaces
whose fumes and choking dust,
drifted down to turn waters
into coagulated, oily streams,
thick and lifeless
as the greed
which fed them.

The seed flowered
and withered;
bearing a single malformed seed of its own
to fall into the tilth
atop a forgotten grave.

Left to itself,
feeble roots started to probe.
Unable to face Autumn's first frost,
it bloomed all too briefly
above the remains of a life
now decomposed,
unable to find the nourishment it needed.

As he did every week,
in hope that mourners would return
with fresh flowers
and quietly murmured messages
washed into graves with tears,
the sexton cleared away remembrances,
already shrivelling and become litter.

One small flower on an unmarked mound
hardly seemed worth the effort of removing.
He left it for the winds of winter
and, by those winds, it was soon lifted.
Petals, leaves, stem and roots
broke free of the earth
and in moments, to the stars were gifted.

Confession

Shadows used to bring security.
They offered safe familiarity
as if by strange osmosis,
everything inside
was always outside.
Diffused and excreted
through the membrane of Being.

Shadows were always there
ready to conceal;
ready to be revealed;
ready to be infused into others
as pure Terror.

But not now.
The shadows in this doorway were no haven.
Not for Jack.
Only for those others, passing to and fro.
Entering the dark portal unshriven.
Leaving free of all blame,
ready, once more, to re-enter their personal Edens,
as yet untainted by fresh sin.

That never happened of course.
It was all in their minds:
a momentarily discomfiting ritual
and the release of relief.
An unburdening of guilt and shame
into the sealed ears of silence,
followed, as always,
by the hollow game of repentance
in anticipation of indulgent wickedness.

➤

What then, of this strange new world?
So much seemed familiar:
the shadows and strange sickly perfumes.
The predominance of red
and visions of blood leaking from wounds.
The need to kneel with head bowed
as if waiting for bullet or blade.
A cannibalistic feast as you washed it down
with a symbolic cup of red wine
for rituals of toasting your victim's fate.

Was this to be Jack's new world?
A world deafened by echoes,
and the cold, wintery silences
of briefly widening eyes
and stifled gasps
on the other side
of a grille?

But what penance or sacrament
could possibly absolve the guilt
of this confessor?

Boxed in

Silence can be frightening, can't it Jack?

Intimidating.

Did you ever see yourself
in the darkness of a lonely space like this
where the penance you seek
is to be shackled
and sweated with memories?

No fists.
No blood.
No voices other than yours?
Where the only inquisitor
is yourself?

Is this a vision of your new world?
You seeking light,
whilst draining the darkness of your soul?

But what else do you hear?
Are they drawing near?
Those insistent whispers,
sliding like oiled steel across your skin,
probing for scars ready to be re-opened?

There's no lock on the door, Jack.
No need for a key.
No way out.
You know the score.

Tell me some more.

In memoriam

Swinging shut behind him,
the door closed
without echoes.

Is this what relief and redemption felt like?
Coldness? Emptiness? Uncertainty?

Still surrounded by shadows,
Jack strode forwards
in search of something more.

What else did he have to offer?
What else to give?

His stride became more certain
as he weaved his way between markers,
mounds and tombstones.

There was no point in kneeling or praying.
He didn't know how.
Instead, he scooped a handful of soil,
muttered three quiet words
and patted the earth back into place.

It wasn't much to leave behind:
just a handful of beads and hope.
But they were all he had.
Now he had nothing.

Just like always.

A solitary soul.

Anniversary

Sheffield Jack
took no crack.
Strung him up.
Skewered his back.
Hung him on a butcher's hook.
Bleeding like a slaughtered pig.
His face, a mask;
a frozen look.
One more carcass for the slab.
Shrivelling now.
Not so big.
Sheffield Jack.
An evil geezer.
Never said he was sorry.
Well, not to me.
Said he'd made amends.
But not with me.
Enough was enough.
I told him – see?
Makes you stop though
when you think about it.
Talk about Fate!
Strange coincidence.
August the eighth.

Happy birthday Jack.

Illustrations not by the author are based on public domain sources:

Front cover ~ John Bearby ~ Unsplash
Back cover ~ Maurice Garlet + Giga Chokhel ~ Unsplash

Darkness descending ~ Ellis Garvey ~ Unsplash
Dark Gods (and Infinite Wisdom #1) ~ j4p4n ~ openclipart.org
Sheffield Jack ~ vadim kaipov ~ Unsplash

www.ingramcontent.com/pod-product-compliance
Lightning Source LLC
Chambersburg PA
CBHW061334040426
42444CB00011B/2914